# GUNS N' ROSES

# TRIVIA BOOK

Uncover The Facts of One of The Greatest Bands in Rock N' Roll History!

**By Dale Raynes**

ISBN: 978-1-955149-22-8

**Copyright 2021. Dale Raynes. All Rights Reserved.**

No part of this book may be reproduced or transmitted in any form or by any means, electronic or mechanical, including photocopying, recording or by any other form without written permission from the publisher.

# TABLE OF CONTENTS

Introduction ................................................ 1

Chapter 1: .............. Troubled Childhoods and Rock'n'roll Dreams ........................................ 3

    Answers ................................................................ 9

    Did You Know? ................................................. 15

Chapter 2: . The Most Dangerous Band on the Sunset Strip ................................... 18

    Answers ............................................................... 23

    Did You Know? ................................................. 30

Chapter 3: ................ *Appetite for Destruction* 33

    Answers ............................................................... 39

    Did You Know? ................................................. 46

Chapter 4: .. Becoming the Biggest Rock Band in the World ....................................... 51

    Answers ............................................................... 57

    Did You Know? ................................................. 64

**Chapter 5:**............The *Use Your Illusion* Years **68**

    Answers ................................................................ 74

    Did You Know? ...................................................... 82

**Chapter 6:**..................... **Collapse of the Titans 85**

    Answers ................................................................ 91

    Did You Know? ...................................................... 98

**Chapter 7:**.....................**Rebirth and Reunion 101**

    Answers .............................................................. 106

    Did You Know? .................................................... 112

# INTRODUCTION

A lot of rock bands are wild. Many of them cultivate that sex, drugs, and rock and roll image. But Guns N' Roses is the real thing, so hedonistic and haunted by demons that they are ready to spin off the tracks at any given minute, as we will see. They did so. Repeatedly.

Many of the questions and facts here will deal with their outrageous lifestyles and seemingly endless capacity for petty and profound feuds. The stories are jaw-dropping, and hopefully, you will enjoy every salacious detail.

But let's not forget why we care in the first place: the amazing music. Sure, everyone appreciates *Appetite for Destruction* for what it is, the perfect debut album. But returning to their music today gives us a remarkable (though all too sparse) body of work. Patience is far more interesting than it seemed at the time. *Use Your Illusion* is not the bloated mess that critics made it out to be. It is a masterpiece. Even the troubled *Chinese Democracy* is far superior to what we had a right to expect. Guns N' Roses is a phenomenal band first—debauched train wreck second.

We are excited that the boys are back together. While we wait for their next album, let's take a trip down memory lane. Do you know rock's ultimate bad boys? Let's see.

# CHAPTER 1:
# TROUBLED CHILDHOODS AND ROCK'N'ROLL DREAMS

1. What is Axl Rose's given name?

    a. John Ferdinand Rose Jr.
    b. William Bruce Rose Jr.
    c. Vernon Axl Rose Jr.
    d. Bruce Ferdinand Rose Jr.

2. How often did Axl go to church as a kid?

    a. Once a week
    b. Two times a week
    c. Three times a week
    d. Up to eight

3. True or False. When Axl was a child, he was never allowed to watch TV.

4. True or False. Axl was an excellent piano player as a child.

5. Axl had a number one role model as a singer growing up and as he perfected his craft. Who was it?

   a. Freddie Mercury
   b. Mick Jagger
   c. Elton John
   d. Steve Tyler

6. Slash was born in England. Where in that country was young Saul Hudson born?

   a. Hampstead
   b. Stoke
   c. Bristol
   d. Southampton

7. At what age did Slash leave home?

   a. 13
   b. 15
   c. 16
   d. 18

8. True or False. At age 13, Steven Adler's mother sent him to Hollywood to live with his grandparents, hoping they could control his bad behavior.

9. True or False. Steven Adler's mother wrote a tell-all book about her son's struggles with addiction called *Sweet Child of Mine: How I Lost My Son to Guns N' Roses*, and he felt betrayed and stopped speaking to her.

10. Slash's mother, Ola Hudson, was a costume designer who worked with music industry heavy hitters. Which of the following rock stars did she have an affair with?

    a. Mick Jagger
    b. Marc Bolan
    c. David Bowie
    d. Lou Reed

11. Slash's father, Anthony Hudson, was an artist and illustrated several classic albums. Which of these records featured artwork by Hudson?

    a. Led Zeppelin – *Houses of the Holy*
    b. Joni Mitchell – *Court & Spark*
    c. Frank Zappa and the Mothers of Invention – *Weasels Ripped My Flesh*
    d. David Bowie – *Hunky Dory*

12. Slash got his famous nickname from a 1960s character actor who often hung around his parents' house. So, which actor came up with the memorable name?

    a. Seymour Cassell
    b. Martin Balsam
    c. Harry Morgan
    d. Harry Carey Jr.

13. Before he discovered the guitar, what was Slash's main childhood passion?

    a. Skating
    b. Biking
    c. Graffiti
    d. Stamp collecting

14. Which member of the band did Slash know the earliest?

    a. Axl
    b. Duff
    c. Izzy
    d. Steven

15. True or False. Axl played in local bands with Izzy Stradlin in their hometown of Lafayette, Indiana.

16. Why did Axl leave Indiana?
    a. To pursue his dreams of being a rock star.
    b. He was unemployed.
    c. He was in trouble with the law.
    d. To get away from his family.

17. What does the name Axl refer to?
    a. A dog
    b. Part of a motorcycle
    c. The name of a band
    d. Axle grease

18. Only one of the original members of Guns N' Roses finished high school. Who is it?
    a. Axl
    b. Slash
    c. Izzy
    d. Steven

19. Where did Duff McKagan grow up?
    a. Los Angeles
    b. Indiana
    c. Seattle
    d. Miami

20. Duff McKagan modeled his look when playing bass on which famous player?

    a. John Entwistle
    b. Phil Lynott
    c. Sid Vicious
    d. Paul Simonon

# ANSWERS

1. B- William Bruce Rose Jr. The singer was born on February 6, 1962, in Lafayette, Indiana.

2. D- Up to eight. Axl hated it. He remembered, "My particular church was filled with self-righteous hypocrites who were child abusers and child molesters. These were people who'd been damaged in their own childhoods and in their lives. These were people who were finding God but still living with their damage and inflicting it upon their children. I had to go to church anywhere from three to eight times a week. I even taught Bible school while 1 was being beaten and my sister was being molested."

3. False. His born-again parents distrusted TV, but he was allowed to watch TV some of the time. "We'd have televisions one week; then my stepdad would throw them out because they were Satanic. I wasn't allowed to listen to music. Women were evil. Everything was evil."

4. False. Though Axl took classes, he never worked hard at it. "I started playing when I was really little, something my father wanted me to do because he regretted that he hadn't taken piano lessons... Sometimes I'd sit there for a couple hours and I'd just

make up things. I think I could have learned how to be a lot better if I'd have been more dedicated."

5. A- Freddie Mercury. Axl has consistently said so. "Queen is the greatest band, and Freddie [Mercury] is the greatest front man of all time," he said in 2018. His importance to Axl cannot be overstated. "If I hadn't had Freddie Mercury's lyrics to hold onto as a kid, I don't know where I would be. It taught me about all forms of music...it would open my mind. I never really had a bigger teacher in my whole life."

6. A- Hampstead. If you said Stoke, you might have read that in an old interview. Even Slash didn't know where he was born until later in life. "I was born in Hampstead on July 23, 1965. I lived in Stoke but was born in London, a detail my dad had to correct me on. We moved to the US when I was six."

7. C- 16. Despite growing up in a privileged home, Slash was more interested in partying and playing guitar. "I was quite a detached kid at home, so I guess I was officially out of the house when I was about 16. But I had always been hanging around the scene in LA because we lived right in the middle of it. At 13, I was cruising up and down Hollywood Boulevard and that whole bit. As soon as I started putting bands together, I started spending long sabbaticals away from home on people's couches and so on."

8. True. You have to wonder what Deanna Adler was thinking! Either way, it didn't work. However, he

would not have met the other band members if he hadn't gone. So we should probably thank her.

9. False. She did release the book. However, Steven, who is trying to overcome his addictions, is supportive. The drummer said, "When you're in a situation where your son or daughter is an addict, you feel like you're the only ones and that everybody else's kids are perfect, and it's just my family and me, but it's not. So, it's a really great book to read and go learn about it."

10. C- David Bowie. Slash was about ten years old. He remembers, "My mum started working with David professionally at first. I'm pretty sure that's how it started. Then it turned into some sort of mysterious romance that went on for a while after that. She did his wardrobe for his whole Thin White Duke period and *The Man Who Fell To Earth* movie that he did. She did all that, and he was around for a while. He was always over – they were always together. I caught them naked once. They had a lot of stuff going on, but my perspective was limited."

11. B- Joni Mitchell – *Court & Spark*. Hudson worked with Geffen Records, which in neat symmetry would later sign Guns N' Roses.

12. A- Seymour Cassel. The actor was well known for appearing in the films of revolutionary director John

Cassavetes. Young Saul Hudson was quite hyperactive. So one day, Seymour grabbed him and said, "Hey, Slash, where ya going? Where ya going, Slash? Huh?" The rest, as they say, is history.

13. B- Biking. The guitarist said, "I was a pro BMX racer as a kid, and my main aspiration was to eventually become a moto-cross champion. I was obsessed! But then I inadvertently picked up the guitar, and everything switched gears inside of 24 hours, and before long, my career took off."

14. D- Steven. The two went to Fairfax High in Los Angeles together, where they became friends due to a shared interest in rock and weed. Slash remembers, "I knew Steven first. Originally, he was a guitarist, and I was going to play bass, but then he went to drums. He moved back home and learned to play drums, moved back, and that's when I met Izzy Stradlin. He came into the music store I worked in to see if I was the guy who'd drawn this picture of Aerosmith he'd seen. He played me a tape that had Axl on it, so Steven and I went along to see him play at Cazares one night."

15. False. As Izzy remembers, "We'd play covers in the garage. There were no clubs to play at, so we never made it out of the garage."

16. C- He was in trouble with the law. Sure, if you said A, you are not entirely wrong. But Axl had a long rap sheet in Lafayette. The singer had been arrested over 20 times on everything from public intoxication to battery. He also served a few months in jail here and there. He served jail sentences up to three months. Finally, Axl was told that he was one false move away from being locked up for good. It's a good thing he moved because Rose would have plenty of false steps. His girlfriend at the time, Gina Siler, remembers, "When I met him, I was having my seventeenth birthday party. He had on a long trench coat, dark glasses, collar pulled up, and said he was trying to stay away from the police. I asked: 'What happened?' He said: 'Nothing. They just always bother me. They always harass me, no matter where I am.' But he would do some pretty wild things. They would go out and drink and do some stupid things, like smash windows along Main Street."

17. C- The name of a band. His first band in LA was called AXL, and he enthusiastically changed his name to that because he loved the name and being in a band that much.

18. C- Izzy. He wasn't exactly a Rhodes Scholar, finishing with a D average.

19. C- Seattle. Duff came from a very different background and place. His first musical experiences came in the pre-grunge Seattle punk rock scene.

Therefore, he has connections with both the glammy LA rock scene and the more down-to-earth Seattle music world. Duff remembers, "In Seattle, I learned a lot from it because everybody had a band, and you'd share gear, share rehearsal spaces, share riffs and bands that you were into — it was very supportive. And I was young - you know, '79 is probably when I went to my first gig, and I was like, what, 14? Formed a band a week later, wrote a song, made a single; it was the first thing I ever did. I sang that song, and my voice hadn't changed yet. So it was a bunch of young people just figuring it out. We weren't 21 — we weren't even *close* to 21. We couldn't go play bars. So you'd play at people's houses or rent a little union hall and throw gigs. It was just a self-supporting, cool fucking scene, with a lot of cool, cool bands."

20. D- Paul Simonon. The iconic bassist from the Clash inspired Duff in more ways than one. He says, "I mean, come on, it's a good look! Whether I look like that or not, I am that guy when I play bass. The way he looks on the cover of the *London Calling* album, where he's about to smash his bass guitar, is just incredible."

# DID YOU KNOW?

- Axl claims that he remembers being molested by his birth father as a baby. However, he did not recognize the events until adulthood, when he reexperienced the traumatic events through regression therapy. The singer recalled, "I remember a needle. I remember getting a shot. And I remember being sexually abused by this man and watching something horrible happen to my mother when she came to get me." He believes that these events led to some of the singer's anger, misogyny, and homophobia issues. "I feel that child abuse and sexual abuse...is kind of the key to why there are so many problems in the world today. The more books I read on it, and the more work I do on trying to overcome the problems that I had in my childhood that I accepted... I knew it was crazy, but I accepted it as normal behavior for my life, and I realize now that it wasn't normal behavior, and it's caused me to act in many ways because it's what I was trained, it's what I was taught, it's what I saw. My formative years were very ugly."

- Unfortunately, his stepfather was not much better. While he did not sexually abuse Axl, he allegedly did so to his sister Rose. He also allegedly beat both children severely. The singer says, "My stepfather is one of the most dangerous human beings I've ever met. So it's very important that he's not in my life anymore or in my sister's."

- Axl's father was murdered, and the singer did not know about the event for years. Instead, he was raised by his stepfather, a devout Pentecostal preacher. The troubled father disappeared in 1984 and did not show up for his parole hearings. A warrant was issued for his arrest. An individual murdered him after sleeping with his wife. The son of the murderer (Charles) testified, "As Charles and his father entered the parents' bedroom, Charles saw his mother on top of the victim engaging in sexual intercourse. After entering his parents' bedroom and witnessing his mother on top of the victim, Charles saw the defendant push his mother off the victim and stab the victim once in the chest with the knife. The victim fell out of the bed and the defendant dragged the victim into the bathroom and placed him in the bathtub. Charles testified that the victim was still alive at that point in time. The defendant then had Charles retrieve a baseball bat. After obtaining the baseball bat, the defendant closed the bathroom door and beat the victim with the bat for what Charles approximated to be two to three minutes. The defendant and his wife then wrapped the victim's body in a painting canvas and moved the body from the bathtub to the garage, where they placed the body in the trunk of the defendant's Ford LTD. When the body was placed in the trunk,

Charles did not detect any sign of life." The body was never recovered, but the Illinois authorities convicted the murderer. Axl did not find out about any of this until years later.

- Slash grew up in such a musical house that it almost seems inevitable that he would eventually become a musician. The guitarist says, "My dad was the rebel of the family; he went to art school, married a black woman, and was part of the whole rock'n'roll scene. LA was the place to be, so moving there made perfect sense. From day one, it was all about the Stones, The Yardbirds, Cream, and The Kinks. And I have to bring The Moody Blues into it because they had quite a strange effect on me. Then when I moved to the States, it was all about bands like The Doors. My mum was into lots of eclectic music, from Phoebe Snow to The Commodores, David Bowie to Led Zeppelin. Both my parents were in the music business, so I was around it 24/7."

# CHAPTER 2:
# THE MOST DANGEROUS BAND ON THE SUNSET STRIP

1. How did Slash get his trademark hat?

    a. It was a gift.
    b. He borrowed it and never gave it back.
    c. He bought it at a flea market.
    d. He stole it.

2. True or False. In his early days in Hollywood, Axl often had to live on the streets for lack of money.

3. What was the name of Izzy's first band in Los Angeles?

    a. Naughty Women
    b. The Atoms
    c. LA Guns
    d. Bazooka Joe

4. True or False. Duff lived across the street from Izzy in Hollywood, and that is how they first met.

5. The first band that Slash and Axl were in together was called Hollywood Rose. So why did they fire the band's founding member, Chris Weber?
    a. A fight over drugs
    b. Musical differences
    c. Chris got mad at Axl for being late.
    d. Axl got accidentally hit in the head.

6. Which Hollywood Rose song later appeared on *Appetite for Destruction*?
    a. "Rocket Queen"
    b. "Anything Goes"
    c. "Mr. Brownstone"
    d. "You're Crazy"

7. Slash, Steven Adler, and Duff played together in a short-lived band. What was it called?
    a. Road Crew
    b. The Farts
    c. Fastbacks
    d. 10 Minute Warning

8. While playing for Hollywood Rose, Slash got sick of waiting around for the big break and auditioned for a hair rock band. Which of these bands rejected him?
    a. Ratt
    b. Warrant
    c. Poison
    d. Cinderella

9. What was the name of the Chinese restaurant in West Hollywood where LA Guns and Hollywood Rose would often play?

   a. Madam Wong's
   b. Mr. Champion
   c. Hui Tou Xiang
   d. Xiang La Hui

10. Early in the band's career, they rented a place at 1139 N. Fuller Avenue (right off Sunset Boulevard). The place had a terrible reputation. What was it called?

    a. The Cat House
    b. The Mad House
    c. The Sleaze House
    d. The Hell House

11. True or False. The guns part in Guns N' Roses is named after original guitarist Tracii Guns.

12. Which of the following bare essentials was not available at the house at 1139 N. Fuller Avenue?

    a. Air conditioning
    b. A bathroom
    c. A functioning door
    d. A kitchen

13. During their early days, the band would often frequent Rage, a gay bar in West Hollywood. Why did they go there?

    a. They were experimenting sexually.
    b. They played there often.
    c. To get free drinks.
    d. To get cheap food.

14. Who was the dominant songwriter in the band in their earliest days?

    a. It was a united effort.
    b. Izzy
    c. Slash
    d. Axl

15. What is the song "Night Train" about?

    a. A type of wine
    b. A type of drug
    c. A sex act
    d. An actual train

16. True or False. The song "My Michelle" is about a real person, and they didn't mind the song coming out, despite its negative narrative about them.

17. Guns N' Roses were signed by Tom Zutaut, a scout from Geffen Records. So, in which LA club did he spot them?

    a. The Troubadour
    b. The Roxy
    c. The Whisky A Go-Go
    d. Starwood

18. True or False. Axl slept with Tom Zutaut's girlfriend after he discovered the band.

19. The first release by Guns N' Roses was an EP called *Live ?!*@ Like a Suicide*. Where was it recorded?

    a. The Troubadour
    b. The Roxy
    c. The Whisky A Go-Go
    d. Starwood

20. In one of their earliest shows opening for a big act, Axl got turned away by security for being late. Duff and Izzy had to sing, and they couldn't remember the lyrics. Who was the headliner that night?

    a. Ted Nugent
    b. The Red Hot Chili Peppers
    c. Alice Cooper
    d. Cheap Trick

# ANSWERS

1. D- He stole it. "I went into this 'in' store on Melrose (Place) in Los Angeles and saw a top hat and was like, 'Oh, that looks cool.' And we had a show that night, so I was definitely looking for something to wear for the show that evening." He walked out with it on his head and never paid for it. Ironically, it was stolen years later, and the police recovered the hat. Oh, and the belt he decorated it with? He stole it from the same store.

2. False. Although he referred to it in some interviews, it does not appear to be true. Axl and his girlfriend lived at 1921 Whitley Avenue in Hollywood. Gina Siler remembers, "There were times when he would take my car to practice. I would help him do his make-up. No, he didn't live on the streets entirely. I helped him out quite a bit. I don't think he likes to think about that, though. There were times, granted when he lived on the streets after I'd kick him out because I got tired of trying to support the both of us, and I got tired of fighting. I would describe the two of us as putting a nuclear warhead in your living room and hitting it with a hammer, and just waiting. That was what the two of us together were like."

3. A- Naughty Women. They were a drag band, and Izzy, a country boy from Indiana, didn't really know

what was going on. His first show ended in extreme violence. "So these guys with no hair turned out to be skinheads, and they hated us. They threw beer bottles and spit. They got on stage and broke the guitar player's finger, trashed the amps, beat the shit out of the singer. That was my first gig. We were called the Naughty Women. At the time, I thought they must have it together because they had business cards."

4. True. Duff recalled, "Izzy [Stradlin] when he lived across the street from me in Hollywood, looked like Johnny Thunders. So I was like, 'Okay, Johnny Thunders guy, perfect.' And when I saw Slash's ad in the paper... His name was Slash. I put it with Slash Records, right? So I was thinking, here's a punker dude like me who's looking for the next thing."

5. D- Axl got accidentally hit in the head. Guitarist Chris Weber hit Axl on the head accidentally during a show.

6. B- "Anything Goes." The song appeared on a Hollywood Rose five-song demo. Then, after a protracted legal battle, it was released in 2014 under the title "The Roots of Guns N' Roses." Weber remembers that the first time they played the song at a show, "It was really loud and aggressive and kind of took people by storm."

7. A- Road Crew. Incidentally, the other three names are bands Duff played for.

8. C- Poison. Boy, that would have changed rock history. Slash recalls, "I couldn't handle it anymore, and I walked. That was right after the first time Axl, and I ever worked together. Matt, the original guitar player for Poison, who was actually a pretty cool guy, had gotten his wife pregnant, or they were getting married or something like that. He was moving back to Pennsylvania. He goes, 'You should try out for Poison.'" However, when the band asked him about wearing makeup, Slash knew it wasn't going to work out. "As I was walking out of the audition, C.C. DeVille was walking in. He had on pancake makeup and a ton of hairspray. I actually remember thinking right then, 'That should be the guy.'"

9. A- Madam Wong's. Esther Wong, who ran the restaurant, was known as the "godmother of punk." That is the spot where Tracii Guns met Axl. Tracii recalled, "Do you guys want to play with us at Madame Wong's West? So I was like, 'Sure, let's do a gig together.' And so we were down there during the day, pulling our crap in for soundcheck, and there's Axl by himself at the microphone, just wailing. I'm like, 'Holy shit, that guy can sing!' That's when I wanted to be close to Axl when I saw him sing like that." The Ramones and the Police also

played there. Unfortunately, the iconic spot closed in 1987.

10. D- The Hell House. The house earned its name both due to the band's conditions and the horrible things that happened there.

11. True. The guns part is for Tracii Guns, and the roses part, for Axl. Tracii said, "We had a singer that our manager didn't like, so we fired him. So then I asked Axl to join LA Guns, and he was in the band for about six, seven months. The same manager ended up hating Axl, and he wanted to fire him. We're all living together at this point, and Axl and I sat down and went, 'What are we going to do?' So we both said, 'Fuck that,' and came up with the name Guns N' Roses, which was going to be just a record label that we'd put singles out on." But they soon realized it was an excellent name for a band.

12. Trick question. It was missing all of the above. Izzy charitably described the place as "a fucking living hell."

13. A- It was a united effort. Though Axl had the most dominant personality, everyone's ideas were heard. Marc Canter was a friend who was often around. He says, "A lot of the songs would start with some idea from Izzy like 'My Michelle' — the spooky intro part of 'Michelle' was total Izzy, but without Slash, we

wouldn't have gotten the harder riff that followed it. Axl would hear these unfinished songs and just know exactly how to work within them. Duff and Steven would then make the songs truly swing and really flesh them out with their ideas. You could say, as some have, that Axl was the most important, [but] if you took any one of those guys out of the equation, it would have drastically changed all of those songs. It was truly a democracy in the beginning; at that time, in 1985 or 1986, they were all on the exact same page."

14. D- To get cheap food. The band discovered they had a $1 buffet at the club. They had some serious financial troubles at the time. Axl said, "We tried to live off $3.75 a day, which was enough to buy gravy and biscuits at Denny's diner for a buck and a quarter, and a bottle of Night Train for a buck and a quarter, or some Thunderbird. That was it. You survived."

15. A- A type of wine. The band went to visit friend Lizzie Grey, who lived on Palm Avenue. Slash remembers, "More than a few sleazy chicks lived there, a few junkie girls we knew lived there." Lizzie passed around a bottle of Night Train, a potent form of wine. After leaving, the band members started to scream, "I'm on the night train!" The following day, the band had the entire song done.

16. True. Michelle Young was best friends with Slash's first serious girlfriend and had a fling with Axl. So, writing a song about her was kind of her idea. She had told Axl how cool it would be to have a song written about her. But of course, she probably expected it to be a bit more positive. Michelle later remembered, "I heard it when I was at my dad's house. I was in my bedroom [when] Axl called. He would always call me and sing me new songs. He would play this drumbeat on his knee and sing and snap to me on the phone whenever he had a new song; he would call me and sing a little and ask my opinion of it." This time, though, she didn't know what to say. "I was so out of it at the time, I was always high back then, so when I heard it and heard the lyrics, I was like, 'Oh, it's fine, it's cool... do whatever you want.' I didn't really honestly think that the album was going to be that huge or even that that song was gonna be on their album, for that matter."

17. A- The Troubadour. It was a lucky spot for Guns N' Roses because they also played their first show at that club. The scout told David Geffen that they would be bigger than Led Zeppelin. Tom remembers that Geffen acknowledged his foresight: "After it hit around 10 million in sales, he called me and told me: 'I thought you were out of your mind when you said they'd be the biggest rock band in the world...but you were right.'"

18. False. However, Tom had that unpleasant experience with another band he discovered, Motley Crue. Singer Vince Neil did that, and Tom found out 25 years later when it was included in a movie.

19. Trick question. It was not recorded live at all. Duff wrote in his book, "It would cost too much to actually record a live record. The crowd noise...is from a 1970's rock festival called the Texxas Jam. We thought it would be funny to put a *huge* stadium crowd in the background at a time when we were lucky to be playing to a few hundred." The EP was recorded at Pasha Studios in Hollywood.

20. C- Alice Cooper. Guns N' Roses opened for all the acts mentioned on their early tour. Unfortunately, however, this catastrophic show took place at Arlington Theater in Santa Barbara.

# DID YOU KNOW?

- The Hell House may have been incredibly seedy, but it is also where the band crafted their trademark sound. They wrote "Welcome to the Jungle," "Think About You," and "Out Ta Get Me" in that house. Duff remembers, "We rehearsed a lot of hours." The place had surprisingly good acoustics as well. The bassist remembers that in the small space, "Our shitty gear sounded magical, clear and *huge*."

- Tracii Guns was not bitter that things didn't work out with Guns N' Roses. He says, "Slash really had an image together and really was like almost like an alien coming in and saving the world. You know what I mean. It was really...the chemistry is undeniable. When I played in the band, I was still going through my Randy Rhoads influence and trying to grasp how to incorporate those styles and stuff into what I was doing. And Slash was pretty much already playing the way he's maintained his whole career, just like a great blues-rock heavy guitarist. And that's exactly what the band needed. I don't believe that the band would have been what it is today if I had stayed in that band." LA Guns continues to record and tour, with Tracii as its leader.

- The period of the band living together in that small house was ended by a severe incident, allegedly involving statutory rape. A 15-year-old girl who had been at the house ran naked onto the Sunset Strip. Axl said, "This hippie chick wandered in and started fucking with our equipment trying to break stuff... So eventually, she wound up running down Sunset naked, all dingy, and didn't even know her own name." However, apparently, there was a lot more to the singer's involvement with the underage girl. Slash wrote in his autobiography, "My memory of the events is hazy, but from what I remember, she had sex with Axl up in the loft. Towards the end of the night, maybe as the drugs and booze wore off, she lost her mind and freaked out intensely. Axl told her to leave and tried throwing her out. I attempted to help mediate the situation to get her out quietly, but that wasn't happening." The cops came to find Axl and brought everyone in the house outside, aside from Axl, who was hiding. Axl later said, "While the cops are out there harassing everybody, asking their stupid questions, I'm with this girl behind the amp, and we start going at it," he later boasted. "That was the rush! I got away with it! It was really exciting." However, Axl and Slash had to hide because they were now wanted for statutory rape. Eventually, the charges were dropped. Whatever happened, the band showed no concern for the girl involved.

- Guns N' Roses shot out of nowhere and took over the rock world with their debut album to the outside world. However, the band was unsigned for years and struggled to break through in the competitive LA scene. Their reputation as troublemakers seemed like an asset later on down the line. However, in the early years, it looked like it may doom their budding careers. Slash recalled, "We'd been together since '84, and got signed in '86, so from then until '87 seemed like a fucking eternity. No one wanted to work with us; we had the worst reputation, we freaked everybody out who met us."

# CHAPTER 3:

# *APPETITE FOR DESTRUCTION*

1. The original artwork for the debut album was pretty gruesome, involving the aftermath of a rape. Why was it changed?
    a. The band had second thoughts.
    b. Geffen wanted to avoid controversy.
    c. It violated obscenity laws.
    d. Many important outlets wouldn't carry it.

2. Which member of Kiss was initially slated to be the producer of the album?
    a. Gene Simmons
    b. Paul Stanley
    c. Ace Frehley
    d. Peter Criss

3. Which *Use Your Illusions* song almost appeared on the debut album?
    a. "Yesterdays"
    b. "Civil War"
    c. "November Rain"
    d. "Coma"

4. To make the song more radio-friendly, Geffen cut "Sweet Child of Mine" down in length. How much of the song did they cut?

    a. A minute
    b. A minute and a half
    c. Two minutes
    d. Two and a half minutes

5. True or False. Slash wanted the main refrain in "Paradise City" to go, "Take me down to the Paradise City/ Where the girls are fat, and they've got big titties."

6. Which Elvis classic did the band record for the *Appetite for Destruction* sessions?

    a. "Heartbreak Hotel"
    b. "Hound Dog"
    c. "Blue Suede Shoes"
    d. "Jailhouse Rock"

7. "Welcome to the Jungle" is a song about the decadence of Los Angeles. Unfortunately, however, Axl was out of town when he wrote it. So, where was he when he wrote the famous lyrics?

    a. Lafayette, Indiana
    b. Seattle, Washington
    c. Dallas, Texas
    d. Las Vegas, Nevada

8. True or False. The sounds of intercourse recorded on the song "Rocket Queen" were real.

9. "Paradise City" is the only song on *Appetite* with a synthesizer part. Who played the synth?

   a. Axl
   b. Slash
   c. Mike Clink
   d. Izzy

10. *Appetite for Destruction* was mostly recorded at Rumbo Recorders in the San Fernando Valley. So, which unlikely act established the studio in question?

    a. Captain & Tennille
    b. Hall & Oates
    c. Simon & Garfunkel
    d. Crosby, Stills & Nash

11. Legendary producer Robert John "Mutt" Lange was considered to produce *Appetite for Destruction*. So why didn't he produce the record in the end?

    a. He didn't like the music.
    b. The band didn't like him.
    c. There was a scheduling problem.
    d. Geffen wasn't willing to pay him.

12. One of the producers Geffen tried for the album was Spencer Proffer. Though the union didn't last, he had a significant contribution to which song on the album?
    a. "Welcome to the Jungle"
    b. "Night Train"
    c. "Sweet Child O' Mine"
    d. "Paradise City"

13. The producer of the album was Mike Clink. What was the first song he recorded with the band as a test to see if they were compatible?
    a. "Shadow of Your Love"
    b. "Reckless Life"
    c. "Move to the City"
    d. "The Plague"

14. The band wanted to discard one of the songs which made it onto the album. However, Tom Zutaut insisted that it remain. So what is the song in question?
    a. "Rocket Queen"
    b. "Night Train"
    c. "Anything Goes"
    d. "Out Ta Get Me"

15. Why did the band part ways with producer Mike Clink after the debut album?

   a. They didn't like the sound of the album.
   b. A fight over drugs.
   c. He couldn't handle Axl being late.
   d. They wanted to produce their own stuff.

16. Who was the primary writer of the song "It's So Easy?"

   a. Duff
   b. Izzy
   c. Steven
   d. Slash

17. "Mr. Brownstone" is a notorious drug song. What drug is it referring to?

   a. Hash
   b. Heroin
   c. Cocaine
   d. Crack

18. The band had an EP called *Live from the Jungle*, which included tracks recorded at the legendary Marquee venue in London. So which country enjoyed an exclusive release of the record?

   a. Canada
   b. The UK
   c. Australia
   d. Japan

19. After a show in 1987, the band helped a singer from one of the bands they played with escape from the police. So, which singer did they assist in evading the overzealous San Antonio police?

   a. Vince Neil of Motley Crue
   b. Ian Astbury of the Cult
   c. Glen Danzig of Danzig
   d. Sebastian Bach of Skid Row

20. Which publication ranked *Appetite for Destruction* as the greatest album of all time?

   a. *Guitar World*
   b. *Pitchfork*
   c. *Revolver Magazine*
   d. *Kerrang!*

# ANSWERS

1. D- Many important outlets wouldn't carry it. The band was upset because they named the album after the art piece, painted by Robert Williams in 1978. "Ended up on a postcard somewhere, and Axl Rose walks down Melrose or somewhere and stumbles across that fucking postcard, and this thing blows his mind," Williams remembers. "So he sets out to get in touch with me, and it took him a long time. No one had heard of the band before. It had no previous history."

2. B- Paul Stanley. He wanted to change the band's sound too much and had a falling out with Slash. Paul says, "Immediately after my interactions with the band, I started to hear lots of stories Slash was saying behind my back." Stanley shared, "He called me gay, made fun of my clothes, all sorts of things designed to give him some sort of rock credibility at my expense. This was years before his top hat, sunglasses, and dangling cigarette became a cartoon costume that he would continue to milk with the best of us for decades."

3. C- "November Rain." The song was initially recorded in 1986 but was judged to be too soft to be included.

4. B- A minute and a half. They cut the vast majority of Slash's fantastic solo. Axl was not amused. "I hate the edit of 'Sweet Child O' Mine'… There's no reason for it to be missing except to create more space for commercials, so the radio station owners can get more advertising dollars."

5. True. The guitarist said, "'Take me down to the Paradise City where the girls are fat, and they got big titties,' I think that was my original lyric for it, and the other guys changed it," Slash tells us, a smile creeping out from under his ever-present top hat, shades, and curly locks. "We all thought it was funny, but it wasn't going to make it on the album. I think that's how it went."

6. A- "Heartbreak Hotel."

7. B- Seattle, Washington. The singer said about Seattle, "It's a big city, but at the same time, it's still a small city compared to LA and the things that you're gonna learn. It seemed a lot more rural up there. I just wrote how it looked to me. If someone comes to town and they want to find something, they can find whatever they want."

8. True. Steven Adler's girlfriend, Adriana Smith, was hanging around the studio, and Axl asked if she would have sex with him in the vocal booth to create realistic sound effects. She agreed, "For the band and

a bottle of Jack Daniel's." If Adler had a problem with it, he does not appear to have said so. However, the song was written about Barbi Von Greif. As Axl recalled, "I wrote this song for this girl who was gonna have a band, and she was gonna call it Rocket Queen. She kinda kept me alive for a while. The last part of the song is my message to this person or anybody else who can get something out of it. It's like there's hope and a friendship note at the end of the song. For that song, there was also something I tried to work out with various people — a recorded sex act. It was somewhat spontaneous but premeditated, something I wanted to put on the record." Not sure I get the connection, but you can't argue with the results.

9. A- Axl. The song was one of his favorites. It was written while on the bus back from San Francisco.

10. A- Captain & Tennille. Mike Clink picked the spot because it was close enough to Hollywood that the band would show up. However, it was not close enough that the band members would "wander away into the street and into trouble."

11. D- Geffen wasn't willing to pay him. The company didn't really believe in the record and didn't want to pay an expensive producer. So it is an open question if the AC/DC and Def Leppard producer would

have maintained the gritty sound that made *Appetite* such a classic.

12. C- "Sweet Child O' Mine." When the band first tried to record the song, Axl couldn't remember what to sing during the breakdown part. So he just said, "Where do we go now?" Proffer told him to sing that line and helped craft that unforgettable section of the song. However, the sessions were a mess. Marc Canter, a friend of the band, said, "GN'R recorded those songs in two or three weeks, at a time when they were totally out of control. Even Axl wasn't in the best shape, and he was the cleanest out of all of them. But he was fooling around with whatever they were doing. Once he saw that they were totally spun out, he just stopped. But nobody showed up on time. They'd throw up or pass out in the studio. But they got the songs done."

13. A- "Shadow of Your Love." The song is a leftover from the Hollywood Rose days. Steven Adler remembers that it was the first song he played with Axl: "The first song we played in rehearsal was 'Shadow of Your Love,' and Axl showed up late. We were playing the song, and right in the middle of the song, Axl showed up, and he grabbed the microphone and was running up and down the walls screaming. I thought, 'This is the greatest thing ever.' We knew right then what we had." Though the song did not appear on an album, it reached #5 on the Billboard Charts as the B-Side for *It's So Easy*.

14. C- "Anything Goes." Axl said at the time, "We [used to do it] so fast. Then wrote another version about our times at the old studio, and we kept that for a while. But then, when we came down to record it, we didn't want to. But Tom was very adamant about wanting that song recorded, so we figured, 'We're gonna have to rewrite it.' In pre-production, we came up with something we liked a lot better, but the verses weren't written until the night we recorded the song."

15. Trick question. The band and producer did not part ways. In fact, it is amazing how well the producer handled the difficult band. Mike doesn't like to get into specifics, but he explains, "A producer needs to become a mediator, if necessary. A band can be a very fragile collaboration within itself. There may be strife between the guitar player and the vocalist or the bass player and the drummer that plays out. A producer needs to be able to work through all those issues without taking sides to help get the project accomplished more easily." He continued to work with the band for several albums and with Slash for years after that.

16. A- Duff. He gave an interview explaining, "It's an account of a time him [West Arkeen] and me, and also the rest of the band, were kinda going through. We didn't have money, but we had a lot of hangers-on and girls we could basically live off of. Things

were just too easy. There's an emptiness; it's so easy." Sounds really tough, Duff.

17. B- Heroin. The drug was starting to take over the band's lives at that point. The band's former publicist, Arlett Vereecke, said, "Slash once told me, 'You know, you do heroin once, and it's such a high that you want to do it again. The problem with that is, the minute you do it a second time, you're addicted to it."

18. D- Japan. Strangely enough, the EP does not feature "Welcome to the Jungle." It did, however, come with the controversial original *Appetite for Destruction* artwork.

19. B- Ian Astbury of the Cult. "Guns N' Roses go on to do the show – they're the opening act… Axl does whatever Axl does every night, which I'm sure includes a few swear words, a few mother-Fs, and this and that. Nothing. Astbury goes on stage, we do our set, he doesn't utter one swear word because he never does. But he's got an English accent, right? So we come off, these cops come backstage, and we kind of lock the dressing room door because we have rumors that the cops want to talk to Ian, and this is not a good thing. And they're not like these days' cops that usually come and tell us how much they enjoy the band… In the old days, we were considered dangerous. So they come in after

Astbury, and Ian climbs out of the Cult dressing room window, which is on the first floor, with a baseball hat on, climbs down the drainpipe, gets on Guns N' Roses' tour bus, and leaves with them."

20. D- *Kerrang!* The hard rock magazine summed up the charm of the album: "They might have inhabited the same genre and clubs as the poodle rockers, but ideologically Axl and co. were poles apart. Exploding the '80s 'me, me, me' bubble with menacing broadsides from the desperate gutters of LA, Guns N' Roses brought a real sense of danger to music. They were five scumbags playing the greatest songs in rock history held together by a volatile chemistry that the band – once it began to unravel – would fail to match. Seventeen years on their gloriously nihilistic calling card still sells 9,000 copies a week."

# DID YOU KNOW?

- The band has consistently been dismissive of "Sweet Child O' Mine," arguably their biggest hit ever. On different occasions, they called it "filler" and "circus music." They had a prejudice against ballads, which is hilarious considering that Guns N' Roses has recorded some of the best-loved rock ballads of all time. However, Slash has made his peace with the song. He says, "You know, what happens is, you come up with something you think is cool, but how it's going to translate to other people, you never know. I was the guy who initially was not a big fan of 'Sweet Child O' Mine' back in the day. That was more not because of the riff, it was really more about the type of song it was at the time because we were a pretty hard-driving band, and that was sort of an up-tempo ballad-y type of a thing. So, it's grown on me over the years, but that's a riff that I never knew was going to take off the way it did."

- Many people involved in the creation of the album were surprised that the band members survived the recording. The fact that they managed to record a superb album was an even bigger surprise. Tom Zutaut was the band's most prominent defender at Geffen. But even he had serious concerns about their self-destructive behavior. "There are some bands that just can't be stopped, and you can sense it. No amount of alcohol or drugs will slow them down. Guns N' Roses were able to consume those things, yet deliver at a live show and deliver in the studio. I don't know if that makes them like gorilla glass on a cell phone or what, but there are plenty of bands that probably did less heroin than Guns N' Roses and drank less alcohol but imploded. For every Guns N' Roses or Motley Crue that delivers, there's probably ten bands that are great but fall apart before they even become successful." However, Zutaut believes that this was a big part of their success. "There was nothing contrived about Guns N' Roses. They lived the life, they were what they were, and everything they did was out of a musical passion and a musical desire to achieve their own vision, which was different than a lot of other people's vision. They were the real deal, and people loved them for it."

- Producer Mike Clink had a good career after producing *Appetite for Destruction*. Among the albums he made was Megadeth's incredible *Rust In Peace*. However, he never could get out of the shadow of the Guns N' Roses blockbuster. "The huge success of Guns N' Roses was great," he says, "but one of the most frustrating things that I had to overcome was assuring bands that they wouldn't end up sounding like Guns N' Roses. I would ask, 'Do you sound like Guns N' Roses now?' When they'd answer no, I'd say, 'Why do you think my end production is going to sound like them?' Sarah Kelly does not sound like Guns N' Roses. Neither does Whitesnake. I take time to help develop an artist's sound. Some bands may sound similar, but there is no 'Mike Clink sound' other than what I bring to the table to make a record as good as it can be."

- *Appetite for Destruction* was the best-selling debut album of all time. In fact, with the 30 million copies it sold, it is one of the best-selling albums of all time. Period. However, it wasn't a great success right off the bat. It slowly made its way to 200,000 copies despite heavy promotion from Geffen, and they were considering ceasing promotion of the album. However, touring and continued airplay turned it into an absolute smash hit. One of the main problems was that MTV would not play the videos of the album at first. Zutaut remembers, "MTV was afraid that if they played GN'R, they would get thrown off of local cable TV channels. It was absurd because I knew this band would get such a huge boost if we could only get the video played. So I asked David Geffen if he could help me out and get MTV to play 'Welcome to the Jungle.'" Alan Niven, the band's manager, said that they had an interesting solution to the problem. "There was an incredibly gorgeous girl who worked with us, and she promised she would dance naked on MTV President and CEO Tom Freston's desk if they would play 'Jungle.' We went at them with a full-court press. At the same time, I sent a blistering letter to the head of programming about what they were playing and what they weren't because I thought, 'F--k. They haven't even looked at this video for six months. Are they ever going to view it?' And bless his heart, the man took it in a very amused spirit, and that turned his head around."

- The band almost broke up while warming up the Rolling Stones. Axl is a fan of the great band and told the LA Times before that show, "We have lots of influences, but the Stones are most definitely a big part of it." The singer asserted, "As a band, we haven't seemed to wear out the Stones yet. We keep learning more and more from them...about the fact you are able to do anything you want in your music." But on the day of the concert, Axl announced he was leaving and wouldn't sing. Axl did not show up. Manager Alan Niven somehow got the LAPD to bring the singer to the venue. According to writer Mick Wall, Niven said, "I want you to immediately send two no-questions-asked uniforms to this address, get the occupants out of that condominium in any which way they can, and bring them right here – in handcuffs if necessary." Sirens wailing and all lights ablaze, the police car sliced through the evening traffic. However, that might not have been the best idea. Axl fell off the stage and then said, "I tried every other fucking way. And unless certain people in this band get their shit together, these will be the last Guns N'

Roses shows you'll fucking ever see. Because I'm tired of too many people in this organization dancing with Mr. Goddamn Brownstone." Mick Jagger couldn't pass up commenting on the train wreck that proceeded him and said, "I think Axl did a good show, but I wish he'd just shut up and play."

# CHAPTER 4:

# BECOMING THE BIGGEST ROCK BAND IN THE WORLD

1. The first side of the album *G N' R Lies* had four songs. The band Guns N' Roses wrote only one. Which song was it?

    a. "Reckless Life"
    b. "Nice Boys"
    c. "Move to the City"
    d. "Mama Kin"

2. The band was on tour as *Appetite for Destruction* became an international sensation. During the tour, they bumped the band they were opening for off the cover of *Rolling Stone Magazine*. Which band was slighted in this way?

    a. AC/DC
    b. Def Leppard
    c. Motley Crue
    d. Aerosmith

3. In 1987, Axl Rose was arrested for assaulting a security guard. The band did not return to the city where it happened for almost 20 years. So which city suffered the long Guns N' Roses boycott?

    a. Atlanta
    b. Houston
    c. Detroit
    d. Minneapolis

4. In 1991, Axl jumped off the stage and assaulted a photographer. Which city banned Guns N' Roses for life as a result?

    a. Boston
    b. Newark
    c. St. Louis
    d. Phoenix

5. Axl got into another fight in 1987. This time, he was enraged when a fan compared him to another singer. So who is the singer you should not compare Axl to?

    a. Vince Neil
    b. Jon Bon Jovi
    c. David Lee Roth
    d. Dee Snider

6. True or False. The first single from the *Lies* album, "Patience," hit number one off the momentum of *Appetite for Destruction*.

7. What did Axl hate about the acoustic sessions for *Lies*?

    a. The production
    b. The lack of energy
    c. The songs
    d. His voice

8. What was the Guns N' Roses song to feature Steven Adler on drums?

    a. "Patience"
    b. "Civil War"
    c. "Rocket Queen"
    d. "November Rain"

9. The cover of the *Lies* album looks quite a bit like the cover of one of John Lennon's albums. So which album does it resemble?

    a. *Imagine*
    b. *Double Fantasy*
    c. *Some Time in New York City*
    d. *Mind Games*

10. True or False. One of the band's opening acts challenged Axl on stage for his racist lyrics in "One In a Million."

11. True or False. *Rolling Stone Magazine* trashed *Lies* as a quick money grab by the band and Geffen Records.

12. In 1988 Guns N' Roses played a festival where two fans were trampled to death. At which festival did this tragedy occur?

    a. Rock in Rio
    b. Monsters of Rock
    c. Glastonbury Festival
    d. Pinkpop Festival

13. Steven Adler was fired from the band. What prompted it?

    a. His excessive heroin use
    b. Conflicts over royalties
    c. Axl being late to shows
    d. His attempts to quit heroin

14. Which member of the band was upset that Steven was fired?

    a. Axl
    b. Slash
    c. Duff
    d. Izzy

15. When he was still in the band, Adler saved the life of which Motley Crue member?

    a. Vince Neil
    b. Mick Mars
    c. Nikki Sixx
    d. Tommy Lee

16. The band once taped up a member of one of their warmup bands and threw him into an elevator. Which band was the unfortunate victim a member of?

    a. W.A.S.P.
    b. Dokken
    c. Faster Pussycat
    d. Warrant

17. In 1989 Axl contributed background vocals to an adult-oriented rock album. Who was the artist in question?

    a. Phil Collins
    b. Don Henley
    c. Robert Palmer
    d. Elton John

18. Slash was once so stoned out of his mind that he ran through a public place naked and was arrested by the police. So what venue did the guitarist streak through?
    a. A mall
    b. A fast-food restaurant
    c. A gaming arcade
    d. A golf course

19. In 1989, Izzy was arrested for urinating in a trash can. Where was the trash can located?
    a. In a parking lot
    b. In a mini-mart
    c. In an airplane
    d. In the street

20. In a show in Paris, Axl went on a rant against a well-known Hollywood actor. So which actor did he trash in France?
    a. Harrison Ford
    b. Warren Beatty
    c. Jack Nicholson
    d. James Caan

# ANSWERS

1. C- "Move to the City." Hollywood Rose originally recorded "Reckless Life." "Nice Boys" was a cover of a Rose Tattoo song. Meanwhile, "Mama Kin" is a cut on Aerosmith's first album.

2. D- Aerosmith. Aerosmith manager Tim Collins recalled, "By the end of the tour, Guns N' Roses were huge. They basically just exploded. We were all pissed that *Rolling Stone Magazine* showed up to do a story on Aerosmith, but Guns N' Roses ended up on the cover of the magazine. Suddenly, the opening act was bigger than we were."

3. A- Atlanta. Axl says he saw the guard assaulting a friend of his. Axl tried to go on with the show but was taken away in a squad car. The singer says he was given a chance to apologize to the guard and avoid arrest but said "fuck you" instead.

4. C- St. Louis. Axl saw an unauthorized photographer while on stage and could not let it go. He told security, "Hey, take that! Take that! Now, get that guy and take that!" When they didn't do it quickly enough, Axl jumped into the crowd after yelling, "I'll take it, goddamn it!" He hit members of the crowd and security before getting the offending camera. He then announced, "Well, thanks to the lame-ass security, I'm

going home!" He never went back on stage. A long and violent riot commenced, injuring several people. The singer was eventually arrested for inciting a riot, but the judge ruled that he had not started it. The *Use Your Illusion* liner eloquently addressed the riot with the words "Fuck You, St. Louis!" The band was banned from the city but returned in 2017.

5. A- Jon Bon Jovi. The two developed a mutual hatred over the years. Apparently, in 1986 they almost came to blows over harsh words. Both hold grudges. In 2006, Bon Jovi reportedly said, "You know what pisses me off? I was reading this British rock magazine this month, and there was a story about Axl Rose and the $13 million GUNS N' ROSES record that was never made. That motherfucker hasn't made a record in 13 years, and he gets all that attention. You know what I've done in 13 years? A lot. But they have continued to write about the freak show aspect of him. Because he's a recluse. That makes him interesting, right?" Jealous much, Jon?

6. False. The song is considered a classic now. However, it peaked at #4 on the Billboard Charts.

7. D- His voice. He was concerned that it sounded scratchy and almost hoarse from the touring. Axl is a perfectionist when it comes to his voice.

8. B- "Civil War." Adler lasted through *Lies* but did not get far into the *Use Your Illusion* sessions.

9. C- *Some Time In New York City*.

10. True. The act in question is Living Color. Singer Vernon Reid criticized the song for encouraging racism in front of the crowd at an LA show. He told the crowd, "If you don't have a problem with gay people, don't call them faggots. If you don't have a problem with black people, don't call them n*." Axl was not amused and, during the band's set, said, "Before we start playing, [I want to say] I'm getting fuckin' sick and tired of all this publicity about our song. If you still want to call me a racist," Rose proclaimed, "you can shove your head up your fuckin' ass."

11. False. *Rolling Stone* was surprisingly favorable towards an album which, although very good, was far from being an album of new material. It read, "Given that Guns N' Roses could probably release an album of Baptist hymns at this point and go platinum, it would be all too easy to dismiss *G N' R Lies* as a sneaky attempt by the band to throw together some outtakes and cash in on the busy holiday buying season... The good news is that *Lies* is a lot more interesting than that... The calm folk-rock melodies of these four acoustic songs reveal yet another welcome facet of Guns n' Roses. They should also end any further mutterings from the doubting Thomases out there who are still making

snide comments about the band's potential for longevity."

12. B- Monsters of Rock. As in other cases where this occurred, the media jumped to blame the band involved. With the bad reputation of Guns N' Roses, it is not surprising that they got bad press. However, later examinations of the circumstances exonerated the band completely. Rose tried to calm the audience down before the tragedy, and no one in the band was aware of the severity of the circumstances until later.

13. D- His attempts to quit heroin. While Steven certainly had a heroin problem, he was fired while trying to take care of it. As the drummer said, "One day, I just went, 'This isn't cool. I don't wanna do this anymore.' And I didn't realize that if you're doing heroin and then you stop doing it, you get violently sick — violently sick. Like, the inside of your bones ache — the inside of your every bone, it aches so bad, and you just wanna die. And I called my manager, and I said, 'Dude, I'm so fucking sick. I don't understand what's going on.' So he came and picked me up, he took me to this doctor, and the doctor gave me an opiate blocker. Well, you're not supposed to take an opiate blocker while you have opiates in your system or you get even more violently sick." Unfortunately, then he was called in to record the *Use Your Illusion* sessions with the band. "'Dude, I'm so sick. Please, can we just wait one more week? I'm

so sick.' And he said, 'We can't waste the money. We've gotta do this song.' So I go in at A&M Records to record, and I'm so weak and sick," recalled Adler. "I did my best, but I had to play, like, 25 times. So they were getting frustrated. And I kept telling them, 'I'm sick.' And they kept saying, 'No, you're not. You're just fucked up.' And I said, 'I'm not fucked up. I'm sick.' And I got kicked out."

14. D- Izzy. He doesn't like to talk about these sorts of things, but Izzy made clear that he valued Steven's contribution to the band. He said at the time, "the first time I realized what Steve did for the band was when he broke his hand in Michigan... So we had Fred Coury come in from Cinderella for the Houston show. Fred played technically good and steady, but the songs sounded just awful. They were written with Steve playing the drums, and his sense of swing was the push and pull that give the songs their feel. When that was gone, it was just...unbelievable, weird. Nothing worked."

15. C- Nikki Sixx. At least, that is what Adler says. Nikki had long noted that Kickstart My Heart's song was written after he overdosed in 1987 and was revived with two shots of adrenaline to the heart. Adler said, "They didn't do that. I dragged him into the shower with a broken hand and a cast on my hand. I rolled him in, I put the cold water on him in the shower, and I started slapping him in the face with my cast.

And next thing you know, the purple in his face just disappeared. And then right then, the paramedics came in, and they grabbed him out of the shower like a rag doll, dropped him in the living room, and they just pumped his chest with their hands. And that was it. But he got a hell of a good song out of it. It is entertainment, after all."

16. C- Faster Pussycat. Slash said that relations between the bands were not great: "We were civil, not what I'd call friendly." When Pussycat drummer Mark Michals annoyed the band, they taped him up and sent him down to the lobby. Slash says, "The hotel staff dealt with him from there."

17. B- Don Henley. The song he sang on is *I Will Not Go Quietly*. Don had won a lot of credit with the band when they were set to perform at the American Music Awards, and Steven Adler was in rehab. So the Eagles drummer agreed to sit in for Adler. Don remembered, "Fortunately, it was a ballad that we played, not a balls-to-the-wall number." Added Henley, "It was a piece of cake. There was really nothing to it. I think they were kind of rebelling about the whole thing. I understood that very well because I lived through one of those periods. So, in a way, I was reliving my past."

18. D- A golf course. Slash thought predators were chasing him. Understandably, he was determined to

get away whether he was wearing clothes or not. When the police got there, Slash recalls, "I was still high enough that I told the story without a shred of self-consciousness."

19. C- In an airplane. Izzy recalled, "I was drunk in the middle of this bunch of senior citizen types. I was smoking, and the stewardess came over. I told her to fuck herself," Izzy said. "I was drinking so much I had to take a piss. The people in the bathroom... man, it seemed like I waited an hour. So I pissed in the trash can instead. The next thing I know, we've landed, I'm walking out, and I see ten policemen. And I remember thinking: 'Uh-oh! I think I fucked up again.'"

20. C- Warren Beatty. Beatty had dated Axl's ex Stephanie Seymour, prompting the singer to call Beatty "a man who likes to play games ... a parasite ... an old man who likes to live his life vicariously through young people and suck up all their life because he has none of his own ... a cheap punk."

# DID YOU KNOW?

- While Axl has denied being racist, he did admit that he was homophobic when he wrote the controversial lyrics to "One in a Million." Or, as he put it, he was "pro-heterosexual" and "I'm not against them doing what they want to do as long as it's not hurting anybody else and they're not forcing it upon me." Due to the controversy, the song did not appear on the re-release of *Appetite For Destruction*. Duff explained, "One thing about Axl is if you're going to try to compete with him intellectually, you've lost because he's a super-smart guy... He's a super sensitive dude who does his studies. When we did that song, I was still drinking, but he was way ahead of us with his vision of, 'something's gotta be said.' That was the most hardcore way to say it. So flash-forward to now. So many people have misinterpreted that song that we removed it... Nobody got it."

- Steven sued the band over the way they fired him. He believes that they tricked him into signing documents when he was in bad physical shape from withdrawal. The drummer claims, "Doug Goldstein called me into the office about two weeks later. He wanted me to sign some contracts. I was told that every time I did heroin, the band would fine me $2,000. There was a whole stack of papers, with colored paper clips everywhere for my signatures. What these contracts actually said was that the band was paying me $2,000 to leave. They were taking my royalties, all my writing credits. They didn't like me anymore and just wanted me gone. That's why I filed the lawsuit – to get all those things back."

- None of the beefs Guns N' Roses had with other bands are more famous or symbolic than their open spat with Nirvana. The Seattle band symbolized the change in the music business in the 90s, while Guns N' Roses were the elite of the 80s old guard. Interestingly, the spat started when Axl pronounced himself a fan of Nirvana's music. Cobain was uninterested in support from a band he saw as sexist and old-fashioned. Therefore, he moved to create distance between the acts. Nirvana drummer Dave Grohl remembers, "Guns N' Roses was about to do this massive stadium tour with Metallica, and they wanted us to open." Dave Grohl recalled, "So Axl had been calling Kurt nonstop. One day we're walking through an airport, and Kurt says, 'Fuck. Axl Rose won't stop calling me.' I think it represented something bigger. Nirvana didn't want to turn into Guns N' Roses. So Kurt started talking shit in interviews, and then Axl started talking back. It went back and forth like tenth-grade bullshit." The Guns N' Roses singer called Kurt and his wife Courtney Love junkies. He also said, "If the baby is born deformed, I think they both ought to go to prison." The two bands played the 1992 MTV Awards and almost came to blows.

- Axl is well known for being late to shows and starting them late. Anyone who has been to a Guns N' Roses show, especially in their prime, knows what we are talking about. This tendency has given him a reputation as a prima donna. However, it appears to be an anxiety-related problem. Axl said, "That hour-and-a-half or two-hour time period that I'm late going on stage is living hell because I'm wishing there were any way on earth I could get out of where I am and knowing I'm not going to be able to make it. I'm late to everything. I've always wanted to have it written in my will that when I die, the coffin shows up a half-hour late and says on the side, like in gold, 'SORRY I'M LATE.'"

- Slash has been sober for years now. He explained why in an interview from 2019: "There's a bunch of different factors, but the first big signal is when it goes from being fun to being miserable. There's this shift from one to another that you don't see coming. It just sort of happens. At one point, you're doing a lot of drinking and drugs, which was more or less fun, then it becomes a burden and a dependency. It turns in a dark direction. Then you start to see it impact everything in your life. And you struggle on, and then you finally have to come to terms with it and admit it to yourself that you've gotten to a place where you're not happy, and it's not doing you any good. Then you have to take a stand and do something about it. Getting from the nucleus of the idea of it not doing you any good to actually doing something about it seems like it takes forever. It's hard, but I definitely got to a point where I wasn't having fun anymore, and it was having a negative impact on what I do as a musician. On top of that, I had two kids. I was raised in this industry. I was raised in the very liberal '60s and '70s, and so I saw a lot of kids who had parents who were just vacant. I didn't want to be that. I had all these different things coming together to push me to get my shit straight. It was really good. It was one of the most important things I've done in my life."

## CHAPTER 5:

# THE *USE YOUR ILLUSION* YEARS

1. Izzy was demoted during the recording of *Use Your Illusion* and told he would have to settle for lower royalties. However, he did contribute to the album. Which of these songs did he co-write?
   a. "You Ain't the First"
   b. "Bad Obsession"
   c. "Right Next Door to Hell"
   d. "Double Talkin' Jive"

2. The band had a long public feud with a band because Izzy allegedly groped the wife of their singer. So what was the band in question?
   a. Poison
   b. Motley Crue
   c. Ratt
   d. Warrant

3. When Guns N' Roses played the 1992 Video Music Awards, Axl sang a duet with which English singer?
   a. Elton John
   b. Eric Clapton
   c. George Michael
   d. David Bowie

4. Axl has punched a lot of people over the years. Who is the most famous person he decked?

    a. Paul McCartney
    b. Eric Clapton
    c. David Bowie
    d. Mick Jagger

5. True or False. The song "Coma" was written about the time Axl overdosed on pills.

6. The last show Steven Adler played with the band was also the first where Guns N' Roses unveiled material for the *Use Your Illusion* albums. The show was intended to benefit a cause. What was the relevant cause?

    a. Helping farmers
    b. Helping dockworkers
    c. Helping nurses
    d. Helping teachers

7. Which well-known 90s alternative rock lead singer provided backing vocals on several *Use Your Illusion* tracks?

    a. Eddie Vedder from Pearl Jam
    b. Scott Weiland from Stone Temple Pilots
    c. Chris Robinson of the Black Crowes
    d. Shannon Hoon of Blind Melon

8. Axl's marriage to Erin Everly was not a great success. How long after their marriage in Vegas did Erin try to annul the wedding?

    a. Two days later
    b. A week later
    c. A month later
    d. Two months later

9. Axl wrote the song "Right Next Door to Hell" about his next-door neighbor. The two got into a fight when Axl threw something at her. What did he throw at his neighbor?

    a. Chicken
    b. A burger
    c. A pizza
    d. A burrito

10. Who sang the lead vocals on the song "So Fine?"

    a. Matt
    b. Duff
    c. Izzy
    d. Slash

11. The band recorded a music video just days before Izzy left the band. It was his last appearance with the band in public. What video proved to be Izzy's swan song for GN'R?

    a. "Don't Cry"
    b. "November Rain"
    c. "Live and Let Die"
    d. "You Could Be Mine"

12. True or False. The song "You Could Be Mine" was featured on the *Terminator II* soundtrack.

13. Which of these songs was written for *Appetite for Destruction* but released on the *Use Your Illusion* albums?

    a. "The Garden"
    b. "Bad Obsession"
    c. "Back Off Bitch"
    d. "Don't Cry"

14. True or False. The band brought in the London Symphony Orchestra to do the orchestration on "November Rain."

15. How many *Use Your Illusion* albums were sold in the first two hours of release?

    a. 100,000
    b. 200,000
    c. 500,000
    d. 1,000,000

16. True or False. *Use Your Illusion I* sold more copies than *Use Your Illusion II*.

17. Which legendary singer did a guest vocal spot on the "Garden?"

    a. Alice Cooper
    b. Robert Plant
    c. Ian Gillan
    d. Ozzy Osbourne

18. Axl was tripping when he recorded the song "My World." What was he on?

    a. LSD
    b. Ecstasy
    c. Shrooms
    d. DMT

19. The highly touted joint tour with Metallica in 1992 had its share of problems. So, which of these setbacks occurred on that tour?

    a. Axl threw up on stage.
    b. James Hetfield was burned.
    c. There was a massive riot.
    d. Axl sustained vocal cord damage.

20. Gilby Clarke was introduced as Izzy's replacement during the *Use Your Illusion* Tour. Which city saw him play his first gig?

    a. Worcester, MA
    b. St. Petersburg, FL
    c. Biloxi, Mississippi
    d. Fairborn, Ohio

# ANSWERS

1. Trick question. He participated in writing all of them. In fact, he penned "You Ain't the First" and "Double Talkin' Jive" on his own. Therefore, trying to demote his share of the royalties was justifiably seen by Izzy as incredibly disrespectful. He later said, "They were gonna cut my percentage of royalties down. I was like, 'Fuck you! I've been there from Day One. Why should I do that? Fuck you; I'll go play the Whisky.' That's what happened. It was utterly insane."

2. B- Motley Crue. According to Motley Crue singer Vince Neil, "Izzy grabbed her breasts. He kicked her in the stomach while she was pregnant. I was pissed. I said next time I see the guy, I'm gonna kick his ass." Vince punched Izzy at the 1989 VMA's, prompting a good deal of anger from Axl. He told the press, "Any time he wants it, anywhere... He tried to turn around and say the same thing, but you know, the invitation is there. I'm easy to find." Vince retorted, "Axl, if you're watching this, I want to challenge you to a fight. I'm gonna give you the time and then give me the place, and there's no backing out now, buddy. It's time to put up or shut up." However, no fight ever took place. But the song "Shot Gun Blues" includes potshots at Vince Neil.

3. A- Elton John. The performance got caught in the crossfire of the infamous Nirvana vs. Guns N' Roses feud previously mentioned. Kurt decided to get revenge on Axl creatively. "I spat on Axl's keyboard; it was either that or beat him up. I saw his piano there, and I just had to take this opportunity and spit big goobers all over his keyboards." Unfortunately, he committed this act on Sir Elton John's keyboards by mistake.

4. C- David Bowie. The Thin White Duke had hit on Axl's girlfriend (and the muse behind "Sweet Child O' Mine"), Erin Everly. They were at a Guns N' Roses video shoot, and Bowie was a bit overzealous in pursuing Everly. Axl responded with his usual subtlety and punched David and chased him around the set. If you guessed Clapton or Jagger, they were also indirectly involved in the story. Axl said, "I was out doing a soundcheck one day when we were opening for the Rolling Stones, and Mick Jagger and Eric Clapton cornered me. I'm sittin' on this amp, and all of a sudden, they're both right there in front of me. And Jagger doesn't really talk a lot, right? He's just real serious about everything, and all of a sudden, he's like, 'So you got in a fight with Bowie, didja?' So I told him the story real quick, and he and Clapton are going off about Bowie in their own little world, talking about things from years ago. They were saying things like when Bowie gets drunk; he turns into the 'Devil from Bromley.' I mean, I'm not

even in this conversation. I'm just sittin' there. Listening to 'em bitch like crazy about Bowie. It was funny."

5. True. Axl explained, "It's Slash's baby, but I started writing about when I OD'd four years ago. The reason I OD'd was because of stress. I couldn't take it. I grabbed this bottle of pills in an argument and just gulped them down, and I ended up in the hospital. But I liked that I wasn't in the fight anymore. I was fully conscious that I was leaving." However, Axl decided to stick around and finish the album.

6. A- Helping farmers. The show was called Farm Aid, and it was held in Izzy and Axl's home state of Indiana. Adler fell on the way to the stage. Slash remembered, "Steven took a run-up to the drum riser, which is a pretty big platform that's hard to miss, and took flight. I assume he was planning on landing next to his kit, but his depth perception and reflexes were clearly impaired, so he ended up landing about four feet short." The first song they played was "Civil War." However, Steven did not know how to play it. Adler believes it was an intentional ploy to get rid of him: "I believe their strategy was to make my playing sound like this. I believe they wanted me to fuck up on live TV; that would be their evidence. By branding me as an ill-

equipped, crappy drummer, they'd be armed with a sound reason for kicking me out."

7. D- Shannon Hoon of Blind Melon. Amazingly, both Axl and Hoon hailed from Lafayette, Indiana. The singer sang on "Live and Let Die," "November Rain," "You Ain't the First," "The Garden," and "Don't Cry." Blind Melon also toured with Guns N' Roses, and the two bands became friendly. However, the antics of the band sometimes upset Blind Melon. Their guitarist remembers what it was like: "I hated waiting around for Axl every night—that kind of sucked. I saw what I didn't want to be—that's one thing that that tour taught me. People stepping aside because Axl was walking down the hallway. It's like, 'What the fuck? He's just a guy.' There were times when we would want to leave to get to the next show, and we would have to wait for Axl to fly in on the helicopter. It was just always this 'waiting on Axl' thing. It would drive me crazy. But I'm so grateful that we got to open up for them and play to that many people."

8. A- Two days later. "Erin and I treated each other like shit," said Axl. "Sometimes we treated each other great because the children in us were best friends. But then there were other times when we just fucked up each other's lives completely." Unfortunately, there was domestic abuse involved.

9. A- Chicken. Axl claimed, "I live next door to a psycho." However, it may be the other way around. The singer threw a wine bottle and chicken at her and also threw away her house keys. However, he insists, "If I was going to hit her with a wine bottle, she wouldn't have gotten up. I would have become a criminal at that point, wondering what I was going to do next to not get busted over the quivering body in my hallway. I don't know what I represent to her. Gabby wants a big place in my life, and she can't take the rejection." Axl was arrested, but the charges were dropped.

10. B- Duff. Duff wrote the song as a tribute to one of his heroes, Johnny Thunders. The bassist said about Thunders' music, "His influence spans the generations and – think what you will of him – but his songwriting is emotive and powerful. Those songs are what it's all about. His music has risen to the top, and it's totally timeless."

11. C- "Live and Let Die." The song had always been a favorite for Slash and Axl. Slash explained, "It's one of those songs, like "Heaven's Door," that Axl and I have always loved. It's always been a really heavy song, but we'd never discussed it and didn't know that we each liked it. We were talking one night about a cover song, and that came up, and we were like, 'Yeah! Let's do it!' So I went to rehearsal with

Izzy and Matt and Duff, just to see whether we could sound good playing it, and it sounded really heavy."

12. False. The song did indeed appear in the movie, but not in the soundtrack release. The memorable clip features Arnold Schwarzenegger as Terminator. He scans the band and concludes that killing them would be a "waste of ammo."

13. Trick question. They all were. The heavy reliance on earlier material has led some to say that the band was low on creativity during the sessions.

14. False. The band played it with an orchestra at the MTV awards. However, the studio recording featured synthesizers in the "orchestral" part. Axl quite brilliantly arranged them.

15. C- 500,000. Many retailers banned the records for their profanity, including Kmart and Walmart. However, that only added to the mystique. *Use Your Illusion I* alone sold over five million copies in the United States. However, compared to *Appetite for Destruction*, it was a bit of a disappointment.

16. False. Though *Use Your Illusion II* was always slightly more popular. It featured the lead single "You Could Be Mine," which gave it that initial leg up.

17. A- Alice Cooper. Luckily, the veteran singer had long forgiven Axl for not showing up at the Santa

Barbara show. However, Cooper never bad-mouthed the band even after that experience. He said, "I was lean and mean and sober, ready to kick everybody's butt and our opening act was unbelievable. They actually helped us because they really challenged us… They really challenged us to be a better band. And it worked. Can you imagine Guns N' Roses going on and then Alice Cooper? That's quite a show!" So, he was happy to help the band and sing on their album.

18. C- Shrooms. Axl recorded it on his own while tripping. Then, he placed it on the album without even telling the other members the song existed.

19. Trick question, all of that happened. I bet you saw that coming! The tour was a mess. On August 8, 1992, the tour reached Montreal. Metallica singer James Hetfield was standing too close to the pyrotechnic explosives and received third-degree burns. Needless to say, the Metallica set ended early. Guns N' Roses were set to go next. However, they made matters worse. They showed up late (the fans waited three hours for them). Then they stopped playing and left because Axl complained about throat problems. The crowd was somewhat displeased. A riot broke out, and the (very strong) crowd overturned cars in the streets. Slash was upset at the outcome and said, "It was actually a huge issue

for me because I'd lost face with everyone in Metallica."

20. A- Worcester, MA. Dizzy Reed was also introduced into the band at that time as the keyboard player. Support group Faith No More found all the changes in the lineup confusing. Keyboard player Robby Bottum said, "I'm getting more and more confused about who's who in Guns N' Roses, and it's blowing my mind. There's Dizzy and Iggy and Lizzy and Tizzy and Gilby and Giddy. Onstage there's a horn section, two backup singers, two keyboard players, an airline pilot, a basketball coach, and a couple of car mechanics."

# DID YOU KNOW?

- Izzy left the band in 1991 and has often said that one of the primary triggers for his decision was cutting down on the hard drugs. "Once I quit drugs, I couldn't help looking around and asking myself, 'Is this all there is?' I was just tired of it; I needed to get out... When you're fucked up, you're more likely to put up with things you wouldn't normally put up with." Izzy has also cited Axl's lateness to shows and occasional decisions to not appear on stage at all as elements in his decision to leave.

- The one member of the band who did not go off the deep end with drugs was Axl. The band's publicist explained, "Axl wasn't really doing drugs because of the medication he was on. He was not a big drinker either. People have a misconception about that, but he was the clean and mostly sober one, really. He wanted to preserve his voice, and he was serious about it." Zutaut agrees with this. He said, "Axl was the only sober one, and he was surrounded by guys that were either strung out on heroin, drugged out on pills, or in an alcoholic stupor, and that added to some of the friction in the band. Axl didn't want to be around the guys that were all f--ked up."

- The track "Get In the Ring" is hostile to many publications. One of them was *Spin* magazine. The music magazine had been instrumental in the rise of the band's career. However, over the years, the band's relationship with the press in general and *Spin* deteriorated. After rising to the top of the heap, Guns N' Roses began to force media outlets to adhere to strict rules. They wanted to be able to edit all interviews themselves and they forced the outlets to sign a contract. Breach of the stringent contract would result in a $100,000 penalty. Bob Guccione, Jr., the *Spin* owner, published the agreement to embarrass the band. He asked readers to sign the contract and send it to the band's management. Needless to say, Axl was not amused. *Spin* also sent reporters to Lafayette, Indiana, to investigate Axl's past. One of their articles referred to the band as "drug-addicted, paranoid, homophobic, racist, xenophobic, ruthless, violent, a threat to the liberty of the press, and a pain in the ass to almost everyone." Axl's answer came in the song "Get in the Ring." As it went, "Bob Guccione, Jr. at Spin/ What you pissed off cuz your dad gets more pussy than you? Fuck you/ Suck my fuckin' dick." However, Guccione had years of martial arts training and was happy to accept the invitation to fight. Especially if it might sell some magazines. Rose backed off in what one Houston paper called "a great moment in douchebaggery."

- The video for "November Rain" is arguably the most popular music video ever made. At the time, the 1.5 million dollars spent on it also made "November

Rain" the most expensive music video ever made. It was the first video ever to reach one billion views on all platforms. It has over 1.6 billion views on YouTube, the most ever for a rock video. Those are incredible numbers, especially considering it is a confusing 9-minute long epic. The video featured Stephanie Seymour, the model who had become Axl's girlfriend. First, she saves the singer from suicide, and then they get married. Then for some reason, Seymour dies. Along the way, there were several iconic moments, including Slash playing the solo in a field with cameras swooping over his head. The director, Andy Morahan, was in charge of many other music videos, including two other Guns N' Roses songs: "Don't Cry" and "Estranged." However, this was without a doubt his magnum opus.

# CHAPTER 6:

# COLLAPSE OF THE TITANS

1. The band named its cover album *"The Spaghetti Incident?"*. Spaghetti is a reference to what?

    a. Drugs
    b. Sex
    c. Alcohol
    d. Pasta

2. The band played one of the songs that would eventually appear on *"The Spaghetti Incident?"* at the Farm Aid charity concert. Which song did they play?

    a. "Hair of the Dog"
    b. "Attitude"
    c. "Black Leather"
    d. "Down on the Farm"

3. True or False. The band recorded a cover of Charlie Manson's song "Look at Your Game, Girl." However, they never released the song.

4. True or False. Because it was a cover album, *"The Spaghetti Incident?"* did not break the Billboard Top 10.

5. Slash once checked into the Marina Del Ray Four Seasons with one of his pets. What species was the unwanted visitor?

   a. A bear cub
   b. A mountain lion
   c. A chimpanzee
   d. A kangaroo

6. The band started to record a follow-up to *Use Your Illusion*. How many songs did it record before sessions fell apart?

   a. 2-4 songs
   b. 5-6 song
   c. 8-9 songs
   d. 10-12 songs

7. Gilby Clarke was fired not long after the sessions. Who wanted him out?

   a. Axl
   b. Everyone but Slash
   c. The management and Geffen Records
   d. Everyone agreed

8. Slash left after being roped into recording a cover of "Sympathy for the Devil" and then having Axl overdub his parts. What movie was the song recorded for?

   a. *Natural Born Killers*
   b. *Interview with the Vampire*
   c. *Pulp Fiction*

    d. *Shawshank Redemption*

9. Matt Sorum, the band's second drummer, quit Guns N' Roses in 1997. Why did he leave?
    a. Because Slash left.
    b. Because he did not believe in the musical direction.
    c. Because Axl insisted on hiring a childhood friend.
    d. Because he wasn't getting paid.

10. True or False. Axl is the only member of Guns N' Roses who always remained a member.

11. Who was the bassist for Slash's first post-GNR project, Slash's Snakepit?
    a. Mike Inez of Alice in Chains
    b. Ben Sheperd of Soundgarden
    c. Jason Newsted, formerly of Metallica
    d. Tim Commerford of Rage Against the Machine

12. Axl brought in guitarist Robin Finck to try and replace Slash in 1997. Which band was he a member of earlier and again later?
    a. Ministry
    b. Korn
    c. Nine Inch Nails
    d. White Zombie

13. True or False. When Axl replaced Matt Sorum with drummer Josh Freese of Devo, he fulfilled Josh's dream of playing with his favorite band.

14. Bassist Tommy Stinson replaced Duff in 1998. Which legendary 80s band did Stinson play for?
    a. The Replacements
    b. Husker Du
    c. Black Flag
    d. Dead Kennedys

15. In 1999, Geffen put out a live Guns N' Roses compilation called Live Era '87-'93. How did the label determine the songs included?
    a. They didn't ask the band members.
    b. They asked Axl and not the former members.
    c. They asked the former members and not Axl.
    d. They had Axl and the former members give input.

16. The Live Era '87-'93 album has 22 tracks. How many of them feature Steven Adler on drums?
    a. 3
    b. 9
    c. 12
    d. 15

17. In which year did Guns N' Roses begin recording the project that would become Chinese Democracy?

    a. 1996
    b. 1997
    c. 1998
    d. 1999

18. The original sessions for Chinese Democracy fell apart because Axl was unhappy with his songwriting. Who did Axl blame for his crisis?

    a. Himself
    b. Slash
    c. Duff
    d. Stephanie Seymour

19. The longest-lasting lead guitarist for Guns N' Roses, aside from Slash, has been Buckethead. His headgear is affiliated with a fast-food chain. Which chain is it?

    a. McDonald's
    b. Taco Bell
    c. Kentucky Fried Chicken
    d. Pizza Hut

20. Guns N' Roses played their first New Year's Eve show in 2001 (the show started in 2000). Where did they play the show?

   a. Madison Square Garden – New York
   b. House of Blues – Las Vegas
   c. The Hollywood Bowl – Los Angeles
   d. Metro Chicago – Chicago

# ANSWERS

1. A- Drugs. Steven Adler referred to his stash of cocaine as his spaghetti because he stored it next to Italian takeout containers in the fridge. When Adler sued the band, the lawyer asked Duff to address "the spaghetti incident," and the band found that to be quite amusing.

2. D- "Down on the Farm." The U.K. Subs had originally performed the song.

3. False. The band did release the song, though, without crediting it on the album. Inevitably, the decision caused a good deal of controversy. Rose said of the song, "I liked the lyrics and the melody. Hearing it shocked me, and I thought there might be other people who would like to hear it." David Geffen was shocked and said, "I would hope that if Axl Rose had realized how offensive people would find this, he would not have ever recorded this song in the first place. The fact that Charles Manson would be earning money based on the fame he derived committing one of the most horrific crimes of the 20th century is unthinkable to me." When pictures of Axl wearing a Charles Manson shirt emerged, it made things worse. The singer said he was just "trying to make a statement. A lot of people

enjoy playing me as the bad guy and the crazy. Sorry, I'm not that guy. I'm nothing like him."

4. False. Though it sold fewer copies than any of their previous albums, "The Spaghetti Incident?" reached #4 on the charts.

5. B- A mountain lion. Like the guitarist, Curtis the mountain lion was a refugee from the Northridge earthquake, which hit their home. When the staff found out, they decided against evacuating Curtis.

6. D- 10-12 songs. The band came together in 1993 and began recording. At the time, Duff was pretty happy with the results and said, "We've been in for two weeks as a full band with Slash and Axl (Rose) and me, and we go from midnight to five in the morning. With Guns, there's no problems with material. The problem has always been getting us in the same room. So now that we're in there, it's rockin'." Media reports were that the album would come out the following year.

7. A- Axl. It was definitely Axl's idea. The rest of the band were close to the new recruit. The firing also reflected deeper tensions in the band. Gilby explained, "It's really strange because the band is like two separate things. There's the guys, everybody except for Axl, and then there's the band *with* Axl. When we're on the road, we're always together. We

hang out together, just like a band. But that's not including Axl. And then there's the band with Axl. He just kinda comes in and does what he does, puts the vocals on and all that kind of stuff." Axl told the other band members he had no respect for Clarke as a person or a musician.

8. B- *Interview with the Vampire*. 1994 was an excellent year for movies, but a bad one for Guns N' Roses. Slash hated the film and had no interest in the soundtrack's sound, but Axl did not care. To add insult to injury, Axl overdubbed some of Slash's guitar parts with another guitarist. Slash felt that was taking things too far. "That was it — having another guitar player record over me without telling me was as much disrespect as I was willing to handle. I washed my hands of that song, I washed my hands of Guns for the moment, and I focused my energy on my own songs and my own project." Slash called the song "the sound of a band breaking up."

9. C- Because Axl insisted on hiring a childhood friend. The guitarist Axl had used to overdub Slash was Paul Tobias. Tobias had been a member of Hollywood Rose and had co-written "Shadow of Your Love" and "Back Off Bitch", two songs performed by Guns N' Roses. However, Axl's attempts to bring Tobias in to replace Gilby Clarke without consulting the band ran afoul of everyone

else. Matt Sorum called Tobias "the Yoko Ono of Guns N' Roses."

10. False. Technically. In 1996, Axl tired of all the other members. He, therefore, left Guns N' Roses and reincorporated it with himself as the only member. Yeah, we are not sure what that means either. The singer explained, "I'd left and formed a new partnership, which was only an effort to salvage Guns, not to steal it." Slash was also confused and wrote in his book, "I didn't really know what else to do after Axl sent a letter saying that he was leaving the band and taking the name with him under the terms of the new contract. After that, we tried to put it back together."

11. Mike Inez of Alice in Chains. However, after playing on the album, he did not play on the tour, as he went on the road with Ozzy Osbourne instead. He was replaced by James Lomenzo of White Lion and later Megadeth.

12. C- Nine Inch Nails. Finck may not be a household name, but he played for two of the biggest bands of the 90s. When he came to see Cirque du Soleil, he met Axl, and Robin was in the backing band. He remembers working with Axl fondly: "Some of my favorite moments as a guitar player were some nights that didn't even make it to that record. I was tight with the recording team and tight with the

band. We were a close-knit bunch of guys, and we just really had a blast."

13. False. Josh wasn't even sure that he wanted to audition and went out of morbid curiosity. The drummer explained, "I was pretty busy at the time, so I didn't really need the job necessarily," he says. "Then I decided that I should go down there because I wanted to meet him. At the time, no one had seen him for a couple of years, and there were all these rumors. He had become the Howard Hughes of rock 'n' roll, and I wanted to see it. I went down, and I liked him. He wasn't the monster that was painted of him."

14. A- The Replacements. The bassist loved his time with the band. "It was a great gig for me. The people were great to me; they are all still my friends. The way it was left was somewhat unfortunate for me because I got to a place where I couldn't tour anymore because my home situation had gotten to such a degree that I had to stay home and take care of my kids and be a stay-at-home dad. After a while of having to turn down tours from those guys, they had to move on, and Axl got the old band back together." Stinson is a single dad and makes his daughters Tallulah and Ruby a priority.

15. D- They had Axl and the former members give input. But not all the members– just Duff, Slash, and

Axl. However, they did not communicate directly. "The live album was one of the easiest projects we all worked on," Slash noted. "I didn't actually see Axl, but we communicated via the powers that be."

16. A- 3. A full 19 had Matt Sorum on drums. However, you wouldn't know it from the liner notes, classifying Matt as an "additional musician" and Steven as a "main band member." Gilby Clarke suffered a similar fate.

17. C- 1998. Things looked pretty good at first. Tom Zutaut reported that they had 50-60 songs ready to work on. However, as we know, things were not quite that simple.

18. B, C, and D. Slash, Duff, and Stephanie Seymour. The singer said in an interview, they all "did more damage to my ability as a writer. To those three, it was all crap. It beat me down so much. At the time of the (*Use Your Illusion*) tours, Slash and Duff said, 'You're an idiot, you're a loser.' I didn't write for years. I felt I was hindered for a very long time. I was also trying to figure out what I wanted to say, when it's right to be venting and when you're digging a bigger hole. Lyrics on *Chinese* took a long time."

19. C- Kentucky Fried Chicken. He wears a KFC bucket. The eccentric guitarist takes that chicken very seriously. During one of the sessions for *Chinese*

*Democracy*, the band had the news on. There was a report that protestors in Pakistan had burned a branch of KFC. The guitarist yelled, "That's fucking IT!" They've gone too far now! I'm joining the fucking army! They are not going to hit KFC, no fucking way! That's it – I can't record anymore. I'm joining the army – now we really are at war!" He then left the studio and disappeared.

20. B- House of Blues – Las Vegas. The show went well, and Axl was optimistic that the album would be out that year. He said, "Hopefully, we will put out a new single sometime this spring, and then the record's gonna be done in June or shortly thereafter."

# DID YOU KNOW?

- *"The Spaghetti Incident?"* was born during the *Use Your Illusion* sessions. The songs there were long and involved, and Axl was in full perfectionist mode. Therefore, the recording was long and arduous. To have some fun and stay loose, the band played old punk covers. They sounded good, so Guns N' Roses recorded a few of them. There was some debate over whether to include them in an even more extended version of *Use Your Illusion*, possibly expanding the set into three or four albums. When it was time to record *"The Spaghetti Incident?"*, they redid them with new guitarist Gilby Clarke.

- There was no immediate follow-up to *Use Your Illusion* because Axl was unhappy with the material. Even Axl's version highlights his dissatisfaction with the direction of the band. In a blog post written years later, the singer claimed, "I have the rehearsal tapes. There's nothing but Slash-based blues rock, and he stopped it to both go solo and try to completely take over Guns. I read all this if Axl would've put words and melodies on, it could've... I was specifically told no lyrics, no melodies, no changes to anything and to sing what I was told or fuck off." Clarke, the guitarist who replaced Izzy, explained, "Axl pretty much threw a wrench into everything. He didn't like what we were all doing. It's Axl's band, and he runs it the way he wants. And whatever he wants to do is gonna happen. So we can work on songs all year long and come up with 20 songs, but when it comes down to it, if Axl writes ten songs, he'll go, 'I want my ten songs on the record.' And that's what's gonna happen. So as much as we work on 'em, it doesn't mean anything because they may never get anywhere. Slash and I are working on some stuff right now together. It's stuff that we put together for the next GN'R record, stuff that isn't gonna make it now. So we're putting something together. We don't know if this is gonna be a Slash solo album or what it's gonna be."

- Slash claims that Axl owned the rights to the band because he forced all the members to sign a contract to that effect. According to the guitarist, "Axl refused to go on stage one night during the *Use Your Illusion* tour in 1992 unless the band signed away the name rights to the band. Unfortunately, we signed it. I didn't think he'd go on stage otherwise." Axl denied this and said it "never happened, all made up, fallacy and fantasy. Not one single solitary thread of truth to it. Had that been the case, I would have been cremated years ago legally, could've cleaned me out for the name and damages. It's called under duress with extenuating circumstances."

- Slash's *Snakepit* album was not a manufactured attempt to create a supergroup or anything like that.

Instead, it was a relatively organic process of musician friends jamming. The loose atmosphere in the studio was a stark contrast to the mess that Guns N' Roses had become. "I was writing for the hell of it, just doing music indicative of where I was at the moment," he says in the book. "I hadn't grasped the idea of doing a Guns record or what that might be going forward. I was just having a good time with no pressure whatsoever. It was guys jamming together, bonding just through the playing and personalities without the rock-star shit. It was just enjoying playing together." Slash loved it, and it reawakened his love for music in a very difficult time. The guitarist explained, "It really helped me discover why I love what I do. That project was the essential soul-searching that I needed because I felt like I'd forgotten myself over the last two years. It was a shot in the arm for me to rediscover what it is I always knew: Being in a band doesn't have to be so taxing emotionally and psychologically... It can just be all about the playing."

# CHAPTER 7:
# REBIRTH AND REUNION

1. In 2012, the band was rightfully inducted into the Rock and Roll Hall of Fame. Which lineup played at the ceremony?

    a. Steven Adler, Duff McKagan, Slash, and Myles Kennedy
    b. Matt Sorum, Duff McKagan, Izzy, Slash, and Axl
    c. Steven Adler, Duff McKagan, Buckethead, and Axl
    d. Matt Sorum, Tommy Stinson, Slash, Gilby Clarke, and Myles Kennedy

2. Which former Guns N' Roses members were snubbed by the Rock and Roll Hall of Fame?

    a. Matt Sorum
    b. Gilby Clarke
    c. Dizzy Reed
    d. Steven Adler

3. Buckethead was reluctant to join the band as lead guitarist. So how did Axl pursue him?

   a. He gave Buckethead a guitar.
   b. He gave Buckethead a bucket.
   c. He gave Buckethead a doll.
   d. He gave Buckethead a car.

4. Aside from wearing a KFC bucket on his head, Buckethead claims to have a special relationship with chickens. What kind of relationship is it?

   a. He claims to be a chicken.
   b. He claims he was raised by chickens.
   c. He claims he can talk to chickens.
   d. He claims he was born a chicken but now is human.

5. Who was the producer credited, alongside Axl, for *Chinese Democracy*?

   a. Roy Thomas Baker
   b. Mike Clink
   c. Eric Caudieux
   d. Caram Costanzo

6. True or False. Once Axl was completely in charge of the band, he stopped flaking on shows and always showed up for Guns N' Roses concerts.

7. Why did Buckethead leave Guns N' Roses?

    a. He was fired so Slash could return.
    b. He had a personal conflict with Axl.
    c. He had musical differences with Axl.
    d. He was frustrated that the band doesn't finish things.

8. True or False. Geffen tried to bring back Tom Zutaut to get Axl to finish the record. But he would disagree because the singer believed Tom had hit on Erin Everly.

9. True or False. One of the elements delaying the album's completion was that Axl needed approval from his psychic before working with anyone.

10. A soda company promised that when *Chinese Democracy* came out before the end of 2008, they would give everyone in America a free soda. What soda brand was involved in this promotion?

    a. Dr. Pepper
    b. Pepsi
    c. Coca Cola
    d. RC Cola

11. True or False. To get Buckethead to return and finish *Chinese Democracy*, Geffen built a chicken coop in the studio.

12. True or False. *Chinese Democracy* is a joke name, meant to express that the album is taking as long as it is for democracy to come to China.

13. True or False. The Peoples Republic of China banned *Chinese Democracy*.

14. How many studios was *Chinese Democracy* recorded in?

    a. 1
    b. 15
    c. 32
    d. 78

15. Before its release, *Chinese Democracy* was streamed. What platform did the band use?

    a. Spotify
    b. YouTube
    c. Myspace
    d. Apple Music

16. Guns N' Roses began working towards a reconciliation of some of their original members in 2015. Who initiated the process?

    a. Tom Zutaut
    b. Slash
    c. Axl
    d. Duff

17. True or False. Guns N' Roses canceled their reunion tour because Axl broke his foot.

18. True or False. Though they are playing together, Guns N' Roses members still do not talk to each other and communicate through staff.

19. Why was Steven Adler not reinstated into the band?

    a. His drug problems
    b. Axl vetoed it.
    c. Steven didn't want to rejoin.
    d. Health problems

20. Why isn't Izzy involved in the reunion tour and plans for an upcoming album?

    a. He wasn't invited.
    b. He wasn't interested.
    c. Health issues
    d. Disagreements about money

# ANSWERS

1. A- Steven Adler, Duff McKagan, Slash, and Myles Kennedy. At the time, Axl said, "It wasn't painful to not be there. It was a beating to deal with all the pressure of feeling I was supposed to be there and deciding what to do. I try to be respectful about getting an honor or recognition, but I don't really know what the Rock Hall actually is. In my experience with the people who run it, I don't see it having to do with anything other than them making money." However, he later apologized for not attending.

2. B- Gilby Clarke. The former rhythm guitarist was unimpressed with the decision. Gilby commented, "Slash and I had a conversation about it. I said, look, when you think of GUNS N' ROSES, you think of the five guys, and so do I. That's what it should be. But if you're gonna induct Dizzy and Matt, now I feel left out. I mean, yes, Matt and Dizzy made the *Illusion* records, and I would never take credit where credit wasn't due. But who fucking cares who gets in? It's not like anybody gets a dollar for it or whatever."

3. C- He gave Buckethead a doll. A press release stated that "at a 1999 Christmas party at Axl Rose's house, the Guns N' Roses leader, whom he had never met before, presented Buckethead with a gift...a hard-to-

find Leatherface doll no one else had given him." The guitarist confirmed this and said it made him believe, "Axl must understand me somehow."

4. B- He claims he was raised by chickens. If you were wondering when asked why he wears a KFC bucket if he is so close to chickens, Buckethead answers, "Well, the bucket is a tomb for dead chickens." Strange as he may be, Buckethead has released over 300 albums and is a fantastic guitarist.

5. D- Caram Costanzo. Incidentally, everyone mentioned in the answers was the producer of the album at some point. Also brought in to produce were Moby and Martin Glover (better known as Youth).

6. False. Axl continued to be late and sometimes did not go on stage at all for shows. It got so bad that there was a riot at a show in Atlanta after he failed to show up. It was not the first time either. Fans in Vancouver had responded similarly a few weeks before. As a result, the 14 shows remaining on the tour were canceled.

7. D- He was frustrated that the band doesn't finish things. A statement Buckethead released explained he was leaving because of the band's "inability to complete an album or tour." Axl responded that Buckethead was inconsistent and erratic.

8. False. Axl agreed to work with Tom. As to whether or not he hit on Erin Everly, it depends on whom you believe. Tom says he was often put in the middle of the vicious fights between Axl and Erin. Therefore, on one occasion, Tom explained, "I said to her: 'A lot of kids can't help repeating what they grew up with. But we have to try and learn from our parents and do better. I'm not gonna sit here and have you blame everything on Axl anymore because the truth is that if you wanted to get out of this cycle, you could. But it requires you to leave him, or it requires you to stop blaming him. I mean, you guys need to go into therapy or something.' She got really mad at me. So her response was to go back to Axl and claim that I hit on her."

9. True. The singer had a psychic that everyone around Axl nicknamed "Yoda." Zutaut remembers, "There was sort of like a medium/ therapist that did past life, regressive, transgressive therapy – whatever. And she took Axl on a journey through his past lives, if you believe in that kind of stuff. And then that led to Axl meeting Sharon Maynard, the infamous woman who looked at pictures of people and told Axl whether or not he should work with them."

10. A. Dr. Pepper. Axl said, "We are surprised and very happy to have the support of Dr. Pepper with our album *Chinese Democracy*; as for us, this came totally out of the blue. If there is any involvement with this

promotion by our record company or others, we are unaware of such at this time."

11. True. Zutaut explains that he told Buckethead, "It's my job to find out whatever it is that will help you get the best creativity out of yourself." So Tom made it happen. He described it, "He's got his chair to record and a little mini sofa in there, and there's, like, a rubber chicken with its head cut off hanging from the ceiling and body parts. It's totally Buckethead's world. It's like Halloween in the chicken coop: part chicken coop, part horror movie. We built the coop, and then he brought in all his props and toys and put straw on the floor! You could almost smell the chickens."

12. False. Zutaut answered the question: "No. And let me put it this way: it would appear we would almost have democracy in China." Still not convinced, Tom.

13. True. In both senses of the word. The government released a statement that the album "turns its spear point on China."

14. B- 15. They included Capitol Studios, Electric Lady Studios, and Sunset Sound Recorders.

15. C- Myspace. It was a different time.

16. C- Axl. He made the fateful and challenging call to reach out to Slash. The guitarist said, "It was nice

that it happened. I don't know if I would have had the wherewithal to call him, just because I'm introverted, and it might have been hard for me. Not during that initial phone call, but after that, it was really good to be able to get rid of some of the negative baggage that we'd been carrying around for a long time. It'd been 20 years of not talking and letting this bad blood continue to be perpetuated by the media. It turned into something way bigger than what was really going on, so it was good to get past that."

17. False. Axl broke his foot during the first reunion show at the Troubadour. Instead of canceling, they borrowed the throne that Dave Grohl had used when he had similar problems.

18. False. It appears that everyone has matured quite a bit. Duff explained, "The best thing about [the reunion] is that we did reconnect, in a deep way. We're now grown-ass men and can be honest with each other. We're able to communicate and figure shit out."

19. D- Health problems. Steven played with the band on a few numbers, the first time he had since he was initially fired. However, his back problems stopped him from joining a full reunion.

20. D- Disagreements about money. Everyone is pretty tight-lipped about it. But in a deleted tweet, Izzy wrote that it was because the band "didn't want to

split the loot equally." It was a LOT of loot. Reportedly $563.3 million. The third highest-grossing tour of all time.

# DID YOU KNOW?

- The recording of *Chinese Democracy* went on for a decade. The record was way over budget, perhaps more than any other record in music history. In 2004, Geffen withdrew funding of the record. The record company released a statement, which read: "Having exceeded all budgeted and approved recording costs by millions of dollars, it is Mr. Rose's obligation to fund and complete the album, not Geffen's." Sometimes the sessions cost $250,000 a month. Indeed, according to a New York Times report, they had spent $13 million by that point, and the album was still three years away.

- The band's appearance in the 2002 MTV Awards is considered to be a massive failure. LA Weekly ranked it one of the most embarrassing moments in the history of the VMAs. As they put it, "When host Jimmy Fallon announced a surprise guest at the 2002 VMAs, the room buzzed with anticipation. When it was revealed to be GN'R, the place went batshit crazy. Nobody expected, however, to see the fat Elvis version of Axl Rose, sporting a bootleg Oakland Raiders Jerry Rice jersey, sweatpants, and incredibly awful braids. Then, there was Buckethead on guitar. Watch for the disappointed (or perhaps horrified) looks on audience members' faces." You could write a book about the Guns N' Roses' VMA performances.

- Axl denies that he became a recluse. Instead, he says he just didn't want to deal with the media. As he explained, "I go to movies, go out with friends, go to car shows. I have a zoo. My animals (wolves, parrots, dogs, cats) are my buddies. They need lots of love and attention." So why did he have an image as a hermit? "I just didn't go places where media was. I wasn't interested at the time. If the place to go was some restaurant in Hollywood, I went to the Valley. There was so much negativity; I didn't see any way to go public. I felt I was going to be slammed. The rock entertainment world just wanted to sell magazines."

- The closest person to Axl in recent years was the housekeeper and nanny of Stephanie Seymour, a Brazilian woman called Beta Lebeis. She switched to working for Axl and has become the most influential person in his circle. Axl had a lot of anger towards his mother, which allowed her to step in as a surrogate mother. The singer explained, "I've been doing a lot of work and found out I've had a lot of hatred for women," he said. "Basically, I've been rejected by my mother since I was a baby. She's picked my stepfather over me ever since he was around and watched me get beaten by him." Beta says, "When I entered into his life, he started realizing that someone cares about him and loves him. I'm a patient person. I trust him, and he did not trust himself. I'm not a psychologist, but he needs someone to listen to what he has to say, and I'm here for him."

- We don't know what the future holds for Guns N' Roses. We are all delighted to see the classic lineup (sort of) back together. There seems to be a genuine spirit of maturity amongst the members and maybe even a bit of camaraderie. Knowing these guys, it could either all blow up tomorrow or lead to the best damn album released in decades. Half of the joy with Guns N' Roses is how unpredictable they are.

www.ingramcontent.com/pod-product-compliance
Lightning Source LLC
Chambersburg PA
CBHW071458070526
44578CB00001B/383